How to make interesting and nutritious salads.

THE JUNIPER PRESS
1979

First Edition 1979
Reprinted 1979

© David Eno 1979

ISBN 0 903981 14 9

Printed by Gabare Ltd., Winchester.

Imperial measures are used throughout,
for conversions see page 32.

THE
LITTLE
BROWN
SALAD BOOK

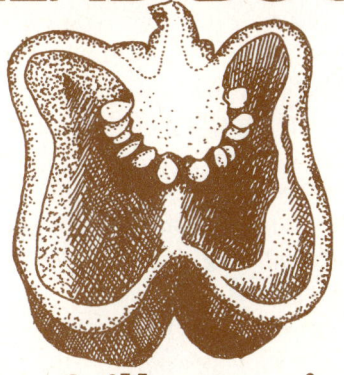

Text & illustrations
David Eno
Calligraphy Jenny Ivermee

Salads can be made from such a large assortment of ingredients that an almost infinite variety is possible. By using each ingredient as it comes into season salads can be made all the year round and because of this seasonal change one need never grow tired of them.

The idea of this book, as with others in the series, is not to limit the readers efforts to the few recipes contained here, but rather to open the way to the readers own creative efforts by giving useful tips information and examples.

The benefits to health of regularly eating fresh, uncooked food can be considerable and it is well worth getting into the habit of eating some raw food each day, even if this requires an effort at first.

To begin with, the vitamin content of these raw foods is higher than in cooked foods. Consequently one can improve ones intake of these 'vital' nutrients, which keep the chemistry of the body functioning normally and help protect against infection and illness.

Secondly the roughage or fibre content of raw food tends to be higher, which is not only beneficial to teeth and gums, but is vital to the effective working of the digestive system, preventing certain types of ulcer, constipation and other disorders which may have far reaching effects on the rest of the body.

Thirdly raw foods tend to be filling while not containing large quantities of carbohydrate or fat. This makes them ideal not only for slimmers, but also for the the rest of us who eat more than we really need.

Lastly by increasing the proportion of raw food in the diet we can be sure of reducing the amount of food additives and toxins we take in.

How to Use Salads

One of the easiest ways of introducing more salads into your normal diet is to serve them either as starters or side dishes with your usual meals. When combining salads with other dishes consider the overall effect. For an already complicated main course a simple bowl of green salad may be all that's necessary and where a number of salad dishes are to be used, as hors d'ouvre, for a main course or for a buffet or pic-nic try to make each bowl as individual yet as simple as possible. Variety really does add much of the spice in cooking and much of the enjoyment of eating a well prepared meal is to find at each mouthful a completely different experience.

Kitchen Equipment

The most basic equipment is a chopping board, a peeler or peeling knife and one or more very sharp cooks knives. Some form of grater is essential, the normal hand type is quite adequate for small quantities, but for anyone who is going to feed regularly on salad I would recommend a rotary hand grater and shredder, (a number of types are now available), or for frequent entertaining the slicing and shredding attachment for a kitchen mixer.

A salad shaker is also a cheap and very useful item for drying lettuce and other leafy vegetables.

Ingredients

Where salt and pepper are called for sea salt and freshly

ground black or white peppercorns are preferable. Oil and
vinegar are frequent require-
ments in salads and their
dressings. Here it is worth obtain-
ing some really good cold pressed olive or sunflower oil. Ground-
nut oil which is the cheapest
and most commonly available
has a poor flavour and adds
nothing to a salad. White wine
vinegar has the finest flavour
and is best for salad use, although
herb vinegars are also excellent.
    The following lists some of
the fresh ingredients which
can be used.

Green Vegetables

Lettuce, watercress, savoy cabbage, white and red cabbage, Chinese cabbage or Chinese leaves, chicory, endives, mustard and cress, American cress, corn salad, dandelion (forced and blanched) celtuce, Brussels sprouts, and the young leaves of spinach, kale, sprouting broccoli (including the heads), seakale beet, good King Henry, celery, turnips, spring onions, nasturtium and sorrel.

Root Vegetables and Tubers

Raw carrot, beetroot, swede, turnip, celeriac and parsnip make delicious grated salads, while in cooked form they can be marinated or otherwise dressed. In addition potato and Jerusalem artichokes can be used in a number of ways.

Peas and Beans

Peas are particularly good raw in salads, as are young broad beans. Peas, broad beans, French and runner beans can also be cooked and eaten cold with various dressings and all dried beans can be cooked and eaten in the same way.

Fruits

Almost all fruit can be used in salads, in particular tomato, pepper, apple, orange, peach, avocado and pineapple which deserves a special mention because its sweet sharp flavour blends particularly well with other salad ingredients. Dried fruits such as raisins, dates and apricots are also good.

Nuts and Seeds

Nuts such as hazel, peanut, almond and cashew and seeds such as sunflower, pumpkin and sesame can be used raw or are especially good lightly roasted with a little salt and vegetable oil in a shallow tray. The smaller seeds take only a minute or so in a moderate oven whilst the nuts take from five to ten minutes and should be checked frequently to avoid burning which happens all to easily.

Herbs

Herbs should be considered an essential part of a salad and the thoughtful use of a few herbs can completely transform even the simplest meal.

Only fresh herbs are really suitable for use in salads. While parsley, thyme, sage and marjoram are available in the winter it is easy enough to grow these and many others in pots on a well lit kitchen window sill through the winter.

For salads the following are most useful :- parsley, thyme, mint, chives, marjoram, basil, tarragon, chervil and savory.

Dressings

Salad should always be served with some form of dressing. In most cases a simple French dressing is quite adequate. Apart from enriching the flavour of the salad, this helps preserve the vitamin content

French Dressing

This simple dressing can be used on almost any type of salad. The only ingredients are oil and vinegar which must be good quality cold pressed olive or sunflower oil and white wine, cider or herb vinegar. The proportion can be anything from two parts oil to one of vinegar to six parts oil to one of vinegar, which can be shaken together in a bottle before use. Alternatively the oil and vinegar can be served in separate bottles, which allows for individual taste.

Lemon Dressing

Replace the vinegar with freshly squeezed lemon juice in the dressing above.

Mayonnaise

Real mayonnaise can be made at home and is well worth the small amount of effort involved. Full instructions for making it plus a few variations can be found in 'The Little Brown Egg Book'.

Yogurt Dressing

Yogurt makes a good dressing for most salads and can be used plain or with chopped herbs added; chives are particularly good.

Tomato Juice Dressing

Beat together one part tomato juice, one part vinegar and two parts olive oil. Reduce the acidity by sweetening with a little honey or brown sugar and add a generous quantity of chopped chives and parsley.

Oilless Mayonnaise.

This is an extremely quick and easy dressing to make if you have a liquidiser and is much less fattening than real egg mayonnaise. Hard boil two eggs and when cool liquidize with two tablespoons of wine vinegar and four tablespoons of fresh yogurt. Add about half a teaspoon of brown sugar, a small clove of garlic and a little salt. Liquidize for at least 3 minutes to get rid of the lumps.

Salad Preparation - General Points

As with all types of food ensuring the good quality and freshness of the ingredients is one of the most basic steps in preparation. Simple dishes are often the most sucessful if the ingredients are carefully chosen and prepared and well presented. Even if you have to pay a little more for fresh top quality foods the extra is rarely wasted.

Thorough washing is particularly important with foods which are to be eaten uncooked. All vegetables and fruit should be washed under a fast running stream of cold water. This helps to remove not only bacterial spores and the eggs of parasites, but also residues of sprays (if not organically grown) and pollutants from the air. Prolonged soaking is not a good thing as the vitamins and minerals dissolve in the water.

All salad ingredients should be stored in a cool place (4°-10°c) but on no account allow to freeze as this destroys the texture and flavour. To revive lettuce and all leafy vegetables wash under cold water and place in a covered bowl in the refridgerator. After an hour or so the leaves will be crisp and fresh. This also works well with fresh herbs.

Preparation of salads should take place as near to the time of eating as possible to ensure the minimum of deterioration. Only a very sharp knife should be used for leafy vegetables to cause the least bruising and once cut they should be dressed immediately with an acid dressing (containing citrus juice or vinegar) to prevent oxidation and halt enzyme action which destroys the vitamins.

Green Salad

This is the simplest way of serving leafy vegetables and may be used as part of a main-course salad, or as a sidedish for pizza, pasta or almost any other hot dish.

Select from the following:- lettuce, watercress, endive, spinach, chicory, cress, dandelion (blanched) sorrel, cabbage or kale. With plants such as spinach, sorrel and kale, the leaves must be very young to be palatable.

The trick of making the most of this type of salad is to combine two contrasting salad plants ie contrasting in colour texture or flavour and to re-member that some form of simple oil and vinegar dress-ing is essential. Chopped herbs also help to add a special touch.

Watercress and Orange Salad

Throughly wash the watercress and remove the larger stalks. Dress with a few teaspoons of oil and a few drops of vinegar and place in a bowl. Thinly slice an orange and remove peel and pips. Decorate the top of the dish by arranging the orange slices in a circle overlapping each other and sprinkle with chopped mint

Cucumber Salad

The cucumber may be peeled, but there is no real need for this. The skin may be scored with a fork, which gives a decorative effect when sliced. Slice the cucumber very thinly and arrange in a shallow dish.

sprinkle with salt, oil and a few drops of vinegar and then with chopped chives.

Tomato Salad

Firm well flavoured tomatoes are essential. These are easy to come by on the continent but difficult to find in England unless you grow your own. Slice thickly and arrange on a shallow dish. Sprinkle with salt and fresh ground pepper and a little olive or other cold pressed oil and serve immediately. This dish should not be kept hanging about as the salt soon makes the tomatoes soft and watery.

Tomato Halves

Cut in half with a knife using a zig-zag cut and treat as above.

Mushroom Salad

½ lb. mushrooms
1 clove garlic
Juice of 1 lemon
salt and pepper

4 Tbs. Olive oil
1 bunch parsley, chopped

Choose large fresh buttons and slice vertically without removing the stalks. In a small bowl mix the lemon juice with the olive oil and pulped garlic. Pour this mixture over the mushrooms and sprinkle with chopped parsley, salt and pepper.

Cabbage and Apple Salad

White, green or red cabbage heart is shredded finely as in the last recipe. This is mixed with about half the quantity of grated apple, which should be treated immediately with a lemon juice dressing to prevent browning. Season with salt and pepper and a few drops of oil. Garnish with chopped chives, and roasted hazel nuts.

Lettuce and Bean Salad

To a coarsely chopped crisp lettuce add cooked broad beans or cooked dried beans, eg. red kidney beans. Chop half an onion or a few spring onions and a few sprigs of mint. Turn all the ingredients together with French or Lemon dressing.

Beansprout Salad

Mix the beansprouts with any coarsely shredded greens and chopped spring onions. Decorate with a little thinly sliced red pepper and use a French dressing.

Diced mixed Salad.

This salad takes some time to prepare, but is well worth the trouble. The ingredients are variable and a half a dozen or so should be selected from the following:- tomato, pepper, avocado, celery, onion, cucumber, courgette, radish, mushroom, celeriac, young carrot, cauliflower, apple and pineapple. The ingredients are cut as far as possible into ¼ inch dice and are mixed together with French dressing, chopped herbs and a few olives if liked.

Russian Salad

Cooked mixed vegetables such as peas, beans, carrots, turnips, potato, Jerusalem artichokes, asparagus etc., are mixed with a finely chopped onion and a few spoons of mayonnaise. Decorate with chopped parsley.

Greek Salad.

Into a salad bowl put layers of sliced green pepper, firm tomatoes and onion rings. Add a few olives and on top some soft white cheese. Cottage or curd cheese are suitable. Dress with olive oil and a very little vinegar.

Potato Salad

For sucessful potato salad waxy potatoes which don't break up when they are cooked are essential. Recommended varieties are Maris Piper, Jersey Royal, and Pentland Lustre if you can get them. Scrub the potatoes and cook them in their skins, preferably by steaming. When cool peel and dice or slice them. Sprinkle with salt and pepper and a few very thinly sliced pieces of onion, or chopped chives if liked. Pour over mayonnaise and mix with a gentle hand so that the potato is coated without being broken. Garnish with chopped mint or parsley.

Winter Salad

Dice a medium sized cooked beetroot, an apple, a small onion and a celery heart. Toss together in a bowl with plenty of chopped parsley and either French dressing or mayonnaise.

Winter Salads

Although we tend to think of salads as summer fare there are many good things available in the winter from which to make salads. Carrots, swede and other root vegetables, apples onions, winter lettuce, endives, kale, Brussels sprouts, cabbage, cress, parsley and thyme and more can be used to add variety to the winter diet.

Grated Carrot Salad

Grate the carrots finely and season with salt and freshly ground pepper. Dress with a few drops of olive oil and the fresh juice of an orange. Turn throughly to make sure all the carrot is dressed, arrange on a shallow dish and decorate with a few thin slices of orange.

Grated Beetroot Salad

Raw beetroot can be treated in exactly the same way as carrot, although a slightly coarser grater is best. The dressing can be the same and a dramatic effect is achieved by arranging the carrot and beetroot on the same dish.

Apple and Walnut Salad

Core and peel a few sharp eating apples and cut into rings. Dip each ring immediately into a bowl containing lemon juice and then arrange on a shallow dish with some chopped celery and walnut halves. Serve with yoghurt or mayonnaise.

Cole-slaw

This well known salad, although often bought ready made is easy to prepare at home. The chief component is white cabbage and it is essential that this is very finely shredded so that there are no lumpy bits. The coarse grating plate on a rotary grater is ideal for shredding, an ordinary grater is rather hard on the knuckles!

The other ingredients can be varied, but I usually use with a small white cabbage, one medium carrot and a small onion. The carrot should be coarsely grated and the onion very finely sliced and chopped, which can only be achieved with a very sharp knife. The ingredients should be then seasoned with salt and ground pepper and very well mixed

together with the dressing. This
is usually ordinary mayonnaise
although the version with garlic
is also delicious. For a complete
change French dressing can be
used.

Green or even red pickling
cabbage can also be used
with equal sucess and give
interesting effects.

Cauliflower Salad

The slicing plate on a rotary
or electric grater is essential for
preparing this salad. Cauliflower
florets, which must be very fresh
and creamy white, are sliced
very thinly. They should then
be seasoned with salt and pepper
and turned in French dressing
until completely coated. Garnish
with chopped parsley

Marinated Vegetables.

This is a method of serving lightly cooked vegetables cold as a salad dish. The best candidates for this treatment are beetroot, young broad beans still in their pods and French beans, although others could be tried. Vegetables should be lightly steamed. As soon as they soften allow to cool. The beetroot should be diced while beans can be cut into pieces.

While the vegetables are cooking prepare a bowl of dressing as follows. Rub the bowl with a cut clove of garlic. Mix one part of best wine vinegar to three parts olive oil, a small amount of sugar or honey, a little salt and a few whole peppercorns and corriander seeds. Add chopped parsley and into this mixture stir the cooked vegetables. Leave overnight or for several hours stirring occaisionally.

END

Conversions

The following are convenient approximations.

Imperial	American
1 pint(pt., 10 fl. ozs.)	$2\frac{1}{2}$ cups (U.S. standard)
1 cup ($\frac{1}{2}$ pt.)	$1\frac{1}{4}$ cups
1 lb. fat	2 cups
1 lb. flour	4 cups
1 lb. sugar	2 cups
1 lb. rice(uncooked)	$2\frac{1}{4}$ cups
4 oz. rice (cooked)	1 cup
1 lb. beans or lentils	2 cups

Tablespoons (tbs.) and teaspoons (tsp.) need not be altered.

Imperial	Metric
1 lb.	450 g.
$\frac{1}{2}$ lb. (8 oz.)	225 g.
4 oz.	125 g.
1 oz	25 g.
1 pt.	575 ml.
$\frac{1}{2}$ pt.	275 ml.
1 cup ($\frac{1}{2}$ pt.)	275 ml.
1 tbs.	17 ml.
1 tsp.	5 ml.

Other Publications

For a free list of all Juniper Press books write to: The Juniper Press, P.O. Box 23, Winchester, Hants. SO23 9TP